A Wreath for Ona B

Eugene Lesser

Los Angeles 2013

1st edition, 2nd printing
9 8 7 6 5 4 3 2 1

ISBN 978-0-9853400-0-1

Heartfelt thanks to...

Joanna Przybylska Buryn, for your patience and sensitivity
in guiding this book to completion.

Lenny Lesser, for your photographic magic in bringing out
the best in the images.

Pamela Nittolo, for your crucial editorial input
and all-around savvy.

Ona Blossom Lesser, my daughter, died of leukemia on April 18, 1994. Around six o'clock on a Monday morning. She was 22. Several years earlier, in a poem, I had written:

A guy I knew told me that Monday morning
is the best time to die.
"Your friends get that off
and the next day for the funeral.
And you don't fuck up anyone's weekend, either."

Well, that guy didn't know jack, as Ona would have said. Monday morning turned out to be a horrible time to die. He was also wrong about the weekend. So that all of her friends could attend, the funeral was on Saturday, and it fucked up *everyone's* weekend. I still haven't had the heart to write much about it all. A few things. There's a lot more to say. Maybe someday. Ona once said to me, "You're such the writer." I guess it's on me.

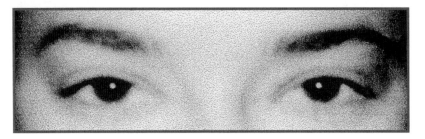

Ona was conceived on Christmas Eve, 1970. I remember Janet, naked, walking out of the bathroom and saying, "I'm ovulating." Exactly nine months later she went into labor. Early in the afternoon on a sunny Indian summer day we drove over the hill to Fairfax.

At the Good Earth we picked up carrot juice and a few other items. We told people there and some people on the street who we bumped into that we were going home to have our baby. Home was on the top of Carson Road in Woodacre. Our rent was 80 bucks a month and the livin' was easy.

We had the incense going. We had flowers all over. We sanitized our towels in the stove. We were ready to have this baby. I had my new notebook and my micro-ball uni medium-point pen nearby, figuring I'd be cranking out your basic epic. Here, in its entirety, is my literary output for the day, my epic:

> *September 24, 1971*
> *2:10 PM contractions start every five minutes for about 30 seconds*
> *4:25   membrane leak*
> *4:40   contractions last one minute, increase in intensity*
> *4:45   remaining waters come*
> *5:13   contractions last 45 seconds*
> *5:23   45 seconds*
> *5:25   40 seconds*
> *5:28   60 seconds*
> *5:32   60 seconds*
> *5:34   75 seconds*
> *5:36   45 seconds*
> *6:15   Malar Flush?*
> *12:21 AM September 25, 1971*
> *Ona Blossom born*

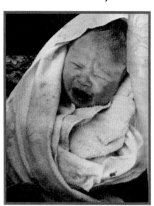

The midwives were magnificent. Dr. Whitt arrived late but hey. I carried Ona into the kitchen, laid her on our huge cutting board and counted her fingers, her toes, checked her out head to foot. OK, we'll take her.

Ona Blossom

Janet says, "A new father has been born."
This is my daughter's second day in the world.
The Giants are one game ahead with three to go.
We've all got a name, a time we were born, and a place.
The commonest thing is to have a baby, to be born.
Every second thousands of people are being born and dying.
That's the farthest out thing of all.
I do feel a closer bond between me and everyone else.
I could go on but I'm hip that you're hip.

1971 was the high point of the San Geronimo Valley's Golden Age.
I was working at the House of Richard 3-4 days a week and took
occasional house painting gigs. On Ona's first birthday I wrote this:

Ona is One

I'm zenning out today.
Today I'm humble and obscure.
I like it so much I may do it again
tomorrow.
Life is simple.
It's so hard to write that.
You can almost break your fingers
trying not to write it.
The truth is hiding in my mouth.
When Ona woke up today, Janet and I sang,
"Happy Birthday to You."
Now Ona can look back on her life like everyone else.
Life is one. Ona is one.

For her first birthday party we invited some friends over. Ona sat
in a highchair and spaced out all night. Terry Tracey brought over his
whole drum kit and set it up right next to where Ona was sleeping.
Lotta music that night. Didn't faze her.

The Minute Waltz

Here I am holding off my daughter with my left arm
while writing this with my free hand.
This might cramp the style of some writers,
but for me it's good.
I write only what is necessary.
I haven't got time for the frills.
She gives me about sixty seconds before
making her move for the ball point pen.
Here she comes, her fat little arms flailing.
(I must write this down.)
I'm holding off my daughter and writing.
Obviously, this can't go on much longer.
What do I need to write?
Here it is: Life is a precious gift.
Don't wait until you have cancer before you get hip to it.
She wants my pen. She fights the good fight
but I persevere. Necessity drives me.
Just one more thing:[1]

[1] *The text is corrupt at this point.*

4

I was 35 and I was a father. I had to become a new person.

Johnny Father: Here and Now

Since I've had a kid my life has dramatically changed.
Used to be when I walked into a restaurant
I'd be thinking of man's inhumanity to man,
or the opening scene of my novel,
or which three females in the restaurant
I'd most like to have sex with.
But now I think:
I hope this place has a high chair.

Janet and I split up a little before Ona's second birthday. That began the routine of seeing Ona only half the time. Long story.

Eugene and Ona

My daughter and I
are hanging out
at my place tonight.
We're eating now.
She puts her foot in the soup. I frown.
My cuff, however, is in my own soup
as I reach across the table to write this down.
We're having a mellow dinner together.
My daughter loves to be ignored while she eats, and so do I.
I don't mind if you talk to me while I eat.
In fact, I enjoy it.
As long as I don't have to look at you. Or say anything.
We're eating my split pea soup (with barley).
Ona picks up a cracker and looks at it with awe.
She doesn't know it's just a cracker.
I tell her it's not cool to throw food on the floor.
She looks at me as though to say, "Oh, really?"
Ona is entering the so-called terrible twos.
I myself am deep into the terrible thirty-sixes.
I try to emulate Ona.
To do my best, to do what I want,
to love openly, to live in the now,
and a few other biggies.
Someday I will be me.
And someday Ona will be Ona.
The split pea soup is great.
Would you like a bowl?

I was writing songs during this period. I tried to capture her lightness
of being in a bouncy ¾ tune.

Ona by Candlelight

Cmaj7   C7
Ona by candlelight,

Fmaj7   Fm6
she's perfect, she's so right.

Cmaj7   C7
Ona, she loves life.

Fmaj7   Fm6
She says it's so nice.

Bm7   E7   Am7 D7
She thinks it's all so funny.

Em7 A7   Dm7 G7
She plays with money.

Cmaj7   C7
Ona, she loves you

Fmaj7   Fm6
and so does her daddy

Cmaj7 C7 Fmaj7 Fm6 C
too.

"Daddy I dreamed a light bulb talked to a person.
Isn't that funny?"
"What did the light bulb say?"
"It said hello and then the person said hello
and then they made love and
the electricity shocked the person."
She giggles.
Who is writing her stuff?
8–4–1976

"What are you doing, daddy?"
"Writing."
"Why?"

I remember, she was three, maybe four, she said,

"Dad?"
"Yeah?"
"Are there just boys and girls?"
"Yeah."
"And that's it?"

Yeah, that's it. No wonder it's so hard.

Ona was spending some time in Hawaii with her mother. In one of Janet's letters from Kauai, she quotes Ona:

> "Send a papaya back to Eugene, okay?
> I wants to tell Eugene about the waves, okay?
> If he gets a new board he can stand up on his new board, okay?
> Let's write some salad to Eugene, okay?"

Ona returned from Hawaii and spent a couple of months with me where I lived on Rock Ridge in Woodacre.

Hangin' with Ona B

It's New Years Eve, 1974.
Ona and I are sitting on the floor before supper,
waiting for the rice to cook.
She's playing with books and marbles,
somehow parlaying them.
I'm playing with pen and paper,
occasionally writing down one of her zingers.
She turns abruptly to me and says, "What are you doing?"
in a way that makes it sound like,
What are you doing with your life?
"I'm writing down the stuff you say."
She likes that.
"Okay, write this down," she says with big eyes.
My pen is poised as she begins.

"This flower is in the sun
on a storm.
On fun.
It is happy.
until it dies.
It is happy when it dies,
except it dies."

She stops and says, "Can I see the words you're writing?"
I show her. She laughs and continues.

"The flower does live for a very long time.
Bees come and take the honey
and butterflies come and take the nectar
until the butterflies die."

Now both of us are drawing.
She's got crayons in both hands
and she's wailing on a big piece of newsprint.
Without stopping or looking up, she blurts out,
"You dumb cowboy."

I tell Ona how much I like her drawing.
She says, "I'll just put some strawberries in it."
Then she flails away with the crayons,
and shows it to me again.
I say, "Now it looks like a flower."
"No," she squeals. "Can't you see the sugar scribbled on?"

Later she says, "Hey Daddy, look at my sun."
I turn and see one of the all-time great suns.
Soon after she says, "Daddy, look at this other sun."
When she notices that I'm ignoring her
so I can write this down, she keeps saying
"Daddy... Daddy... Daddy..."

until finally I turn toward her other sun, knowing that
it was going to be an unforgettable sun.
She gives me the drawing with the two suns.
"Mail it to Janet. She'll love the racing of the suns,"
she says, pointing to some wild purple lines.

"Dad, we're in a coloring book."
"Oh yeah?" I say tentatively.
"Yeah," she says, mimicking me,
and then, "Everybody's coloring us in."

I remember walking in the house one day
and she started laughing and said,
"Daddy, you always come in the house like that."

The rice is done. The table is set.
Before we eat she says she wants to say grace.
Here's Ona's grace:
"Dear Lord.
Thank you for this food.
I like food.
The food is good.
Give it to me.
I'll eat it.
Dear Lord."

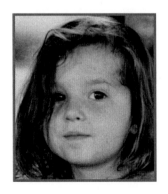

Ona was born in the San Geronimo Valley in Marin County, and lived there her whole life. She went to Lagunitas elementary school with all the other valley kids, and then to high school at Drake over the hill in Fairfax. Ona had remarkably healthy habits. She ate no meat or fish, and abstained from smoking and drinking. The gnawing question remains: How could leukemia invade such a healthy body? Pamela suggested the virulent fertilizer used on the San Geronimo Valley golf course. There are so many environmental disasters that we live with every day. Where do you start?

Ona was diagnosed with leukemia in her freshman year at the Rhode Island School of Design (RISD). A round of chemotherapy put the disease in remission for a couple of years, but it returned to stay. She spent a lot of time at UCSF up on Parnassus Street.

Ona and I were in the solarium on the 12th floor, looking down at the cars on Parnassus and the people walking on the sidewalks and crossing the street. She said, "I wish I could be any one of them." She would've taken on any of their problems because they were all walking around free as a bird, while she was up here in the solarium on the 12th floor.

The final months were very difficult for Ona. Much pain, many weird drugs, and further complications from infection. During her last few hours, Pamela and I were on one side of her bed and Janet and Marty were on the other side. I'm not sure if she was aware of anything. Her face was swollen. When she was declared dead, I kissed her on the lips. They were chapped and cold.

We went to a kind of waiting room where we could just sit down. Finally, we said our goodbyes to Janet and Marty. If it had been in the middle of the night, we could have quietly left the building and gone home. But it was about 8:00 a.m. and the hospital day was in full swing. It was terrible waiting at the elevator with a bunch of others, none of whose daughters had just died, and riding down with people chatting about this and that, as though anything mattered. Pamela and I finally got to our car, and just sat in it for awhile. A friend of ours, a nurse on her way to work at UCSF, who had been checking in on Ona regularly, happened to walk by. She bent over to see through the car window and said, "Hi." We just looked at her and she knew instantly.

Driving anywhere in Marin rubs my nose in it. If I go to visit my friends in West Marin, it's either drive on Route 1 by the Olema cemetery where she's buried or go through the valley where she was born and grew up. I think of her all the time. Sometimes I masturbate just so I won't think of her. I've spent whole days with my throat muscles cramped from keeping back tears, and then, after giving up the fight, not being able to cry.

Whenever Ona and I would drive around the valley or through Samuel P. Taylor Park on the way to Point Reyes, we'd usually sing Sinatra tunes. She knew every word of Frank's *Come Dance with Me* album. "Hey there, cutes, put on your Basie boots..." she'd sing to me, her eyebrows raised. I also dug her throaty vibrato that she sometimes cranked up in parody. She did a slow version of *It Had to Be You* and laid it on thick on the word "you." She was also into Julie London. I had two of her albums and Ona wore out both of them, especially the one with *Cry Me A River*. Although she dug Ella and Sarah and the others, her personal favorite was Julie. She dug Julie London's esthetic: gorgeous but no nonsense.

I think the most memorable times we spent together were singing in the car. We usually looked straight ahead – I was driving, after all – but near the ending, or anytime the lyrics were especially good, or the harmony was a little far out, we'd turn our head toward each other, invariably at the same time, and briefly lock eyes.

At Ona's 8th grade talent show at the Lagunitas School, and without me knowing anything about it, she and her mother trotted on stage and sang a bebop tune, *Donna Lee*, that I had written words to. I was wondering what they were going to do when they got to the line, "She can roll a joint as good as you." So as not to offend, they sang, "She can fry an egg as good as you." It was a kick in the head.

One afternoon we were driving to Fairfax to have lunch. She was 12 and going through puberty and I was giving her my A speech on the whole deal. I told her that, despite the fact that I was her dad and therefore not of the same gender as she or her mother, I was, you know, there for her if she ever needed to talk to someone about, uh, intimate stuff. With a patronizing smile she shook her head up and down. I said, "So if you ever need to talk to someone would you think of confiding in me?" Without hesitating, and without smiling, she said, "No."

I'm dredging up stuff. I just don't want the world to forget her.

I have happy memories of various trips we all took together with Pamela and Lenny. Camping trips, trips to Tahoe. Once Ona brought Madonna's new CD, *Blond Ambition*, with her and we listened to it all week. The four of us had a great trip to New York in 1989. She was 17 and it was the summer before her senior year. We went to Madison Square Garden to see the NBA draft, which fell on my birthday. Lenny, Pam and I were really into the draft, and I was hoping Ona wouldn't be bored. When I asked her if she was having fun, she said, "Are you kidding? Surrounded by lots of young, good-looking, soon-to-be millionaires?"

We also saw *Tosca* in Central Park, then got caught in a heavy rain right as we were walking out of the park. We tried at first to stay as dry as we could, ducking under the occasional store awning, but the rain swirled ferociously under the awning and drove us back out in the open where we decided it wasn't any worse. We finally stopped darting around and slowed all the way to a stroll, laughing our asses off. Thoroughly soaked, the four of us cut quite a figure on the subway back to our hotel. Quite possibly the most fun I've ever had in my life.

Having lunch with Ona was one of my favorite things. She was a severe restaurant critic. If she didn't get exactly what she wanted, she'd send it back until they got it right. And she didn't suffer bad service gladly. Mediocre was not a category. Service, and everything else, for that matter, was good, which is merely what it was supposed to be in the first place, or it sucked.

I just wish we could have lunch together.

First Rain

My daughter used to love the rain,
especially the first rain of the season,
usually in October, sometimes in September,
late September when she was born.
She called me up once when she was
over at her mother's house in Lagunitas.
She said, "I love the first rain. Isn't it beautiful?"
We buried her in the rain last April,
one huge final rain before spring took over.
It started the night before and never stopped.
We were crying and crying,
standing there in the pounding rain and in no hurry.
Tonight is the first rain of the season again,
the first rain since we buried her.
Boy, would I love to call her up right now
and tell her how beautiful *she* is.
I suppose I have to write this.
"You're such the writer," she said.
She would've wanted me to at least try
to tell the world how much she loved the rain.
Especially the first rain.

After O

A stat that we really glom on to
is the average life expectancy.
Males in the US –74.2 years.
Females in the US – 77.6 years.
Whatever.
We believe in it.
There's no God so you have to *believe* in stuff.
It's human nature.
Like having opposable thumbs,
or self-consciousness.
Us guys think we're going to live to be 74.2,
that we've got it coming to us.
But we've got nothing coming to us.
Nothing.

Why?

Kids always ask "Why?"
I did all the time.
I wanted to know the context.
Whenever I asked my father, "Why?"
(I never asked my mother),
he always answered, "'Y' is a crooked letter."
He talked in one-liners like that,
and didn't supply footnotes.
Maybe he knew that answers are always wrong.
I think when I was a kid and asked "Why?"
I really wanted an answer,
but after I became a man, I didn't want to know.
I just wanted to know if there *was* an answer.
Or is "Why?" just another stupid question.
My daughter died a few months ago at age 22.
She used to ask me "Why?" all the time.
Unlike my father, I'd try to explain everything.
Back when I was Atheist Magazine's Man of the Year,
I didn't want God to exist,
just to prove the superiority of my ideas.
Now I'm out of ideas.
I want to know "Why?" again.
And I want my daughter.
I *prayed*, man.
Okay, God, I'll suspend my disbelief.
Humble me. Batter my heart.
Then I find that oh he exists all right
and, by the way, he's some sick fuck.
Oh, so *that's* why.

Driving Out to Olema

Stopping for flowers in Fairfax, I pick out a bright bouquet.
The perky young woman who wraps them for me says,
"You're going to make someone very happy."
"I certainly hope so," I say.

Ona's burial plot is 127A.
I walk around to see the nearby plots.

Right next door at 127 is French Jacks, 1887–1988,
who died at age 100.
The same plot contains his wife, Mabel L. Jacks, 1885–1974,
who died in her 89th year,
and their daughter, Ellen Hill Jacks, 1915–1998,
who died in her 83rd year.

Then comes 126A, Randle Borreson, Jr., 1973–1997.
He was born two years after Ona and died three years after her.

Across the path, at #274, is Michael Pater de Rotte, 1954–1974.
Younger than Ona.
His plot has a home-made wooden cross
made from two 2 x 8 boards driven into the ground.

Nearby is Betty Ann Horick.
July 23, 1922 – February 23, 1993
"Forever with the Lord"

Near Betty is John D. Smith.
"At Rest in God's Care"

Then Charlie Gianini, Flight Officer
A.A.F., 1922–1945
About the same age as Ona.

And Carrie Ann Walther, 1956–1985,
wasn't much older.

Then a plot for a married couple.
The stone says,
Sheila Sheehan, 1930–1992
Gregory Sheehan, 1928–1996
"Sheila, it was a slice of heaven. Greg"

George Skakel
KIA Vietnam
January 12, 1946 – March 6, 1968
Father James Curtis Skakel
Pfc US Army, WWI
11–11–99   12–18–83

Gregory John Maxwell
1962–1971
A Loving Boy

A lot of Rosemary grows at the Olema cemetery.
It grows fast and it takes over an area quickly,
covering up the headstones.
Whenever I go there I bring pruning shears.
Also, a scrubbie to get the grit off of the headstone.

I always sing to her.
I sing the songs we used to sing together.
Cry Me a River, *On Broadway*, and always
You Make Me Feel So Young, just the way Sinatra did it.
Is there another way?
Sometimes I sing it quietly, sometimes loud and in a higher key,
really belting it.
At first I was careful not to sing too loud
in case it bothered someone who might be there.
Funny thing, whenever I've been there,
I've never seen another person.
Great being able to sing to her in a loud voice.

Then I cry, sometimes just a little bit, sometimes a lot.
Then I gather my pruning shears and my scrubbie
and my rags and my hand-shovel and hand-rake
and throw them all in my red plastic bucket
and walk back to the car, taking the same path
through the cemetery that I took
on that rainy day we buried her years ago.

I never asked "Why me?" As far as I'm concerned, there's no point in knowing why. If knowing why would have changed my diagnosis or treatment for the better, then I would have been interested, but it couldn't change a thing, so on to more relevant topics. Besides, there isn't really a "why" unless you make one up.

Sometimes I played with that. I would concentrate on the idea that the reason I was faced with a life-threatening illness was because I was supposed to be exceptional and unique and enlightened and awakened to life. Then it didn't bother me so much – I was kind of getting a leg up on everyone else – an investment in my future, if you will.

I guess that will sound insane to anyone who hasn't been through what I have, and even to a few who've been through exactly what I have. All I can say is I really do like myself better now and I have an awareness of life and a contentedness that I never had before, and Oh, so much more patience. The exciting thing is I know I'll keep growing from it always. So corny, but true.

Ona Blossom, 1971–1994

Made in the USA
Coppell, TX
27 December 2024